CHAMELEON, CHAMELEON

Story by

Joy Cowley

Illustrated with photographs by

Nic Bishop

Scholastic Press

New York

The chameleon rests
in his tree.
His skin has peaceful colors.

He wakes up hungry for a juicy insect.
He looks this way . . .

. . . and that way.

No food! No food!
He must find a new tree home.

Slowly, the chameleon climbs down the tree, step...

by step...

. . . by step.

He stops.
Is something hiding there?

A gecko!
The gecko looks scary,
but it will not hurt the chameleon.

Step by step,
the chameleon creeps
to the ground.

He looks this way . . .

. . . and that way,
watching for danger.

What is this?
It is a tiny chameleon.
It is not dangerous.

What is that?
It is a tiny frog.
The frog will not harm him, either.

Something hangs
from a low branch.
Suddenly, it jumps!

Another gecko!

The gecko will not hurt the chameleon.
The chameleon moves on.

What's this?
A scorpion!

Watch out, chameleon!
The scorpion's stinger
is poisonous.

Carefully, the chameleon creeps past.

At last, the chameleon
finds a new tree.
He is safe again.
He climbs up slowly,

step...

by step...

by step.

Is there food in this tree? Yes!

The chameleon sees a big caterpillar.

ZAP!

Chew, **chew,** **gulp!**

Something is watching.
Another chameleon
lives in this tree.

Her skin is dark
with angry colors.
Go away!

But the chameleon greets her with bright colors.

She sees that
he is friendly.

She welcomes him
with pale colors.

Two chameleon friends . . .

. . . have happy colors.

Did You Know?

The two chameleons featured in this book are panther chameleons from the island of Madagascar, which is rich with strange and wonderful animals. There are geckos that look like moss growing on tree trunks, and others that look like dead leaves on the forest floor. There are tiny poisonous frogs with bright colors to warn other animals not to eat them.

Chameleons come in many sizes, from as large as a big squirrel to as tiny as a matchstick. Male panther chameleons are about fifteen inches long, while females are about eight inches long. Most chameleons live in trees, where they hide among the leaves. They are always very cautious and move slowly, taking one careful step at a time. They have feet like little pincers and long tails to hold tight to branches. Their eyes can look in different directions at once, to check for danger or food.

When a chameleon spots its favorite food, such as a fly, a grasshopper, or a caterpillar, it creeps close, then suddenly spits out its long tongue. Muscles at the tip of the tongue grab the insect as it is zipped back into the chameleon's mouth.

A chameleon always likes to stay safe and it usually avoids others of its kind. But sometimes it will climb down from its tree to look for one with more insects to eat, or to look for a mate. On the ground, it is no longer well hidden, so it stays on the

lookout for forest floor animals. Some, like snakes and scorpions, could be dangerous. Others, like geckos, are harmless. It might even meet a leaf chameleon, one of the smallest chameleons, which is less than three inches long and lives on the leaf litter.

Chameleons are most well-known for being able to change color. People once thought they did this to match their surroundings. But only a few types of chameleons clearly change color, and they do it depending on their mood. For example, a chameleon's colors might darken when it is cold or upset, or they might brighten when it goes to sleep.

Mostly, chameleons change color when they see each other. Males turn bright colors to impress females or scare off other males. Females have their own colors to tell males if they are friendly or would rather be left alone. Chameleons cannot hear sounds very well. So they use color as a way to "talk" to each other.

HOW THE PHOTOGRAPHS WERE TAKEN

Chameleons are extremely shy, sensitive, and complex creatures that require a lot of patient, dedicated care. Captive animals were used for this book because of the large number of photographs that were needed and the many months that were required to take them. To avoid stress, which chameleons are very susceptible to, I had to limit photography to less than thirty minutes on any one day. The rest of my day was often spent capturing their favorite wild insect foods and attending to their many other special needs. On many occasions, a chameleon needed several days to become familiar with its photography setting before any pictures were taken, to ensure that its behavior in front of the camera would be natural and relaxed. A handful of the most complex photographs had to be created in more than one step. For example, because of the unpredictable nature of photographing two animals together, these images were created by first photographing each animal separately and then stitching them together into one scene with many hours of computer work. As with most nature photography, work had to progress at a pace and under conditions set by the subject. But the reward was great, especially to be able to provide for young readers an intimate introduction to these extraordinary and engaging animals.

ACKNOWLEDGMENTS

For helpful advice, I would like to thank Bebe Blu Chameleons and ChameleonCondo, and to extend a special thanks to Reid at Captive Bred Specialties.

LIBRARY OF CONGRESS CATALOGING-IN-PUBLICATION DATA

Cowley, Joy. Chameleon chameleon / by Joy Cowley ; photographs by Nic Bishop.— 1st ed. p. cm. 1. Chameleons—Juvenile literature. I. Bishop, Nic, 1955– ill. II. Title. ;
QL666.L23C69 2005   597.95'6—dc22   2004007291

ISBN: 0-439-66653-8 (alk. paper)

10 9 8 7 6 5 4 3 2 1   05 06 07 08 09

Printed in Singapore   46 • First edition, April 2005

Book design by David Caplan • The text type was set in 27-point Myriad 565 Condensed.